101 Tips for Parenting Teenagers

Or

"Who Messed Up My Kid?"

Kurt Zimmerman

Cover Illustration by Ian R. Ward

www.ianrward.co.uk

email: studio@ianrward.co.uk

DEDICATION

If not for any of my twelve children and fourteen grandchildren, this book would not be possible.

(Nor necessary)

Please enjoy!

ACKNOWLEDGMENTS

Illustrations are licensed by Fotolia.com

The book you are about to read is the one I wish I had read 29 years ago, when my first child turned 13. Since then, I have parented twelve children careening through their teen years, the twilight zone period between thirteen and eighteen years of age.

Whether you think of this time period as 'The Never Ending Story', 'Mission Impossible', or 'Walking Through the Valley of the Shadow of Debt', it is not only possible for you to survive your child's teenage years, but to build a solid adult relationship with them. Humor, consistency and empathy are the keys.

A good friend of mine once shared some sage advice. He was a middle school guidance counselor, and by choice he spent most of his waking hours with hundreds of hormone-soaked bundles of teenage energy. Without a hint of sarcasm, he told me that the best way to weather the teenage storm was to lock them in a closet when they turn thirteen, and not to let them out until they turn eighteen. True story.

This advice illustrates the ongoing frustration in dealing with teenagers. Locking anyone in a closet is, of course, not a viable solution. However, locking OURSELVES in a closet to escape a teenager from time to time is an option that should be kept on the table. These years are full of change, discovery, experimentation, successes and failures. Many of these experiences can be as thrilling or painful for parents as they are for teenagers.

As parents, we think we always need to have the right answer, and have everything figured out. Then life happens. There is no way to plan a perfect response to the unexpected. It is essential to be hard on some things and soft on others. Confident, yet understanding. Accessible, yet discreetly invisible. You need to be as firm as a drill sergeant and as flexible as a yoga instructor. I've discovered that flexibility is better than predictability. You need to use all of the experience you've gathered over the years, but never forget what it was like to be a teenager.

Parenting teenagers is not for the faint of heart and nobody gets it right all the time.

The good news is this: You are already an exceptional parent! In fact, I would guess that you are in the upper percentile of good parents! I say that confidently because you are taking positive measures to improve your parenting skills by shopping for books such as this. This book is by no means the tell all or end all of parenting books, but rather, a collection of useful tips from my nearly thirty years of parenting teenagers.

I would also guess that you are already doing a lot of things right! We all make mistakes, and mine have been mercifully left out of this book, saved for another larger volume to be written later.

Or not.

Below are 101 useful survival tips that will help you avoid some of the mistakes that I made while you make YOUR journey through the teenage years. Whether you are a parent, a teenager, or an innocent bystander, it is my hope that you will find the following pages enlightening and (I hope) a little bit entertaining.

101 Tips for Parenting Teenagers

Surviving Teenagers Tip #1- Imagine a person who is concerned with their friends, their family, how to be accepted, how to pass next week's math exam, what other people think about them, homework, what to wear, the best way to style their hair without getting made fun of at school, what Jimmy Smith might be doing at that very moment, and what they are going to do with the rest of their life. Stressful, right? Cut your teenager a break whenever you can.

Surviving Teenagers Tip #2- Believe it or not, your teenager still thinks you are the greatest. Even when they are yelling at you and telling you how much they hate you. No one can influence them like you can. Set an example for them to follow. Be the person you want your kid to grow up to be.

Surviving Teenagers Tip #3- Don't yell at your kids. As soon as they hear the volume, they will tune you out. What works better is to lean in, and whisper. (It's much scarier.)

Surviving Teenagers Tip #4- When problems arise, decide whose problem it really is. Let kids own their own problems. For example, if you want them to pick up groceries, but they don't have gas for their car, it's your problem. If they want to go visit friends but have no gas, it's their problem.

Surviving Teenagers Tip #5- Don't make a threat you won't or can't carry out. For example: In America, attending driver's training and learning to drive is a big deal; a rite of passage. Driving privileges should only be suspended for irresponsible driving, and not threatened because they didn't clean their room, or didn't do their chores, etc. If they run over the neighbor's mailbox, or drive through the lawn at school, it's probably time to give them a grown up time out and pull their license. At least until they earn enough money to replace the mailbox.

Surviving Teenagers Tip #6- If your teenager is doing chores and asks for a favor, unless the answer is yes, wait until the chores are done before giving them your answer. Otherwise, it is unlikely the chores will get finished.

Surviving Teenagers Tip #7- Resolve to NEVER clean your teenager's room for them. You have raised a perfectly capable person who can do that for themselves. If the room has a door, you can close it and live in the rest of the clean house. Most teenagers really don't care if their room is clean or not, so don't waste your time; they won't appreciate it. Since teens are ALWAYS asking for favors, (Take me here, buy me this, can I go to…) that is when you can get them to straighten up a little before you answer.

Surviving Teenagers Tip #8- Resolve to NEVER pick up a teenager's clothes from the floor. We have a clothes hamper in the laundry room. If the clothes are not in the hamper, they don't get laundered. To some teen boys, this doesn't matter. They have no problem re-wearing yesterday's clothes. Let their friends at school tell them they smell funny. Teen girls seem to prefer clean clothing.

Surviving Teenagers Tip #9- Allow natural consequences to be the teacher. Example: If your daughter decides on extremely short hair, remind them how long it will take for it to grow back, but if they insist on getting it cut, let them get it cut. A few weeks later, when they want you to buy hair extensions, you can remind them of your warning while you are out shopping for a hat.

Surviving Teenagers Tip #10- When you feel like you are going to get angry and yell at your teenager, grab a pencil and bite on it. If you mistakenly choose a pen, it will get ink all over when you bite it in half.

Surviving Teenagers Tip #11- A great quote to remember is from Jeff Bezos- "We are stubborn on vision. We are flexible on details..." This is an especially handy quote to remember when decorating teenager's rooms, or choosing a new pair of glasses.

Surviving Teenagers Tip #12- You don't always have to be the enforcer. For example, instead of insisting that your new driver has to be home by ten, simply remind them that the police will take their license if they are caught driving after ten. (In most states.) New teenage drivers value their license more than a couple of laughs with their friends and will make it home on time. We used this very handy state law to establish our curfew time of 10PM also.

Surviving Teenagers Tip #13- Never let your teen have friends over without getting them to straighten up a little. This is a great lesson in being a good host. Besides, you may never have to put up with their friends again if you make this a rule. Actually, you really DO want to meet their friends, and you may be pleasantly surprised at how well-mannered they are. We decided early on that it was better to put up with the noise, the mess, and the extra grocery bill than to worry about where our kids were. If you supply the pizza, your teenager's friends will tell them what cool parents they have. Another plus, and well worth the price.

Surviving Teenagers Tip #14- ALWAYS remember to NEVER say "always" or "never." There are very few 'absolutes' in the teen world, and you need to keep your options open. Teenagers can feel helpless when you say, "You never do this..." or "You always do that..."

Surviving Teenagers Tip #15- As soon as you allow your teenager to control your emotions, you've lost the battle! (You can practice your straight face and controlled emotions by sending them back to school after the weekend without smiling.) Of course there will be times when they are going to hurt your feelings, but if they see you crying about it, you have given them control over you.

Surviving Teenagers Tip #16- Teenagers can be ruthless. When they are in the habit of badgering one parent for something, try to minimize the time that parent is alone in the car with them. It could turn out to be a long, uncomfortable drive.

"On these long trips, it's vital that
Mommy gets her quiet time."

Surviving Teenagers Tip #17- The opposite of tip #16 is
when you want to have a talk with THEM. They are a
captive audience in the car when you are taking them on a
shopping trip.

Surviving Teenagers Tip #18- Most large requests come from teenagers when only one parent is around. It's the old 'divide and conquer' game. This strategy develops early on and is repeated regularly if it works. Waiting for the other parent, or waiting to think about it before answering is a good habit to develop.

Surviving Teenagers Tip #19- One tactic a teenager uses is "I need an answer right now or I will miss out on _____." If your answer is "I'm really sorry you are going to miss out, because I need more time to think about it" to last minute requests, you won't get them as often.

Surviving Teenagers Tip #20- Driving your teenagers here and there is time consuming. Make sure your teen is prepared to spend an equal amount of time helping you out around the house. Your time is as valuable as theirs. Work out a deal and agree to the details before you agree to drive them somewhere.

Surviving Teenagers Tip #21- This little trick works well. When children are misbehaving in the car, pull over. When they calm down, you can proceed. Obviously, this tactic works better when you are on the way to their friend's house than when you are going to school.

Surviving Teenagers Tip #22- No parent can fix a teenager's broken heart. Don't even try. Just be there to listen, or stay out of the way if requested. If you can get a hug in, you get a big parenting A+. Resist the temptation of piling on if your teenager is complaining about somebody who has inflicted the pain. They may be dating that same person again next week!

Surviving Teenagers Tip #23- What you see as unimportant, your teenager might think of as life-or-death essential. For example, your teenager might believe they will absolutely DIE if they don't get to meet their friends at the mall. You, on the other hand, would never allow your fourteen year old daughter to go to the shopping mall by herself, just to hang out with her friends. Try to reach a compromise. Perhaps you could drive her there and then hang out in the bookstore for an hour, while she sees her friends.

Surviving Teenagers Tip # 24- Teens see everything through hormone-colored glasses.

Surviving Teenagers Tip # 25- Every household has its own 'normal.' Whatever you have allowed in your home up to this point is your teenager's 'normal.' If you yell, fight, argue, swear, smoke, drink, do drugs, gossip, drive over the speed limit, run yellow lights or steal from your employer, that is what is acceptable and normal for your teenager. You have been setting the standard all along, without realizing it!

Surviving Teenagers Tip # 26- Change is always an option when it comes to setting standards in your house. It's never too late to change. You can also usually find some in the couch cushions.

"I'm exploring another revenue stream."

Surviving Teenagers Tip # 27- Each teenager has their own planet where they live, and it is usually not the same planet the rest of us live on. These planets are usually named after the child, by the way. Once you realize that your child is from another planet, and everything else revolves around them, it is much easier to enter into realistic diplomatic discussions.

Surviving Teenagers Tip # 28- The earlier you can teach a lesson, the cheaper it is for them to learn. For example, if you don't take care of your toys, they might get broken. $10. If you don't take care of your car, the motor might seize up. $1800.

Surviving Teenagers Tip # 29- Never say, "I told you so". There are two reasons to resist saying this. The first reason is because it does nothing but make your teenager dislike you. The other reason is they won't remember when you told them in the first place.

Surviving Teenagers Tip # 30- Birthdays are a big deal to a teenager, especially a girl's sixteenth birthday. Take the opportunity to make a big deal out of it and them at the same time. These events show them that they are valuable to the family and to you.

Surviving Teenagers Tip # 31- Christmas is the perfect opportunity to help steer a teenager in the right direction. If your child is interested in photography, buy them a nice camera. If your child is in their twenties, buy them luggage.

Surviving Teenagers Tip # 32- Do whatever you have to do to get your teenager a job. Most teens are willing and anxious to go to work and earn some money that belongs to them. A great place to work after school and weekends is the hardware store. Not one of the big box stores, but the mom and pop hardware store down the street. They will learn how to fix things around the house, and you will get to use their discount.

Surviving Teenagers Tip # 33- I'm really not kidding about the hardware store. In a very short time, they will learn how to fix windows and screens, cut keys, wire a switch and fix plumbing. The most important thing they will learn is, "Yes, Ma'am" and "Yes, Sir."

Surviving Teenagers Tip # 34- A part time job for your teenager is a great way for other adults to teach your kids their most valuable lessons. They will also be able to interact with the general public in a controlled environment. There is something profound about a privileged kid watching a man look at the change in his pocket to decide if he should fix his faucet or eat lunch that day.

Surviving Teenagers Tip # 35- Let your teenagers eavesdrop on your conversations. You can impart your values as you tell your spouse about the time you gave the extra money back when the clerk gave you too much change, or when you left the room when a co-worker started telling dirty jokes. If you sit your teen down to tell them these things, they won't listen, but they will pick it up when you tell someone else.

Surviving Teenagers Tip # 36- The teenager's golden rule goes something like this- "Do unto others the way your parents do unto you." Teens are the best mimics on the planet. Be the best person you can be.

Surviving Teenagers Tip # 37- All teenagers have an ingrained sense of fairness. I think this starts at birth, when one child is playing with a better toy than the other. You can argue until you are blue in the face, but there is no way you will convince a teenager that it is fair they have to clean up a mess they didn't make.

Surviving Teenagers Tip # 38- Most teenagers love to make deals. "I'll do this if you do that." Negotiating skills and being an experienced poker player are great skills to have when raising teenagers.

Surviving Teenagers Tip # 39- If you want a teenager to do something, give them choices. "Would you like to do this now, or later?" Make sure you agree on when later is. You may be thinking this afternoon, they may be thinking after graduation. Close the loopholes.

Surviving Teenagers Tip # 40- The same applies for agreeing on a return time if they are going out. Don't leave the day open-ended. Ask them when they are going to be home, and then remind them of what THEY said if they are late. You will be surprised how reasonable they can be if they are the ones who come up with the time. When you let them make small decisions like this on their own, you are building trust. If they decide on an inappropriate time, you can always negotiate a better time. When they leave the house in the morning, don't assume they are planning to return before dark.

Surviving Teenagers Tip # 41- Once your teenager is in high school, they should be responsible for getting their homework done on their own. It is perfectly okay to ask if they had any homework before they go out, and if they do, agree on when they are going to be home to get it done. The morning of the next day of school is not an agreeable time, by the way.

"I didn't think of it as someone else writing my term paper, I thought of it more as a guest blogger situation."

Surviving Teenagers Tip # 42- If your teenager tells you that they need thirty no-nut snacks by second hour as they are heading out the door for school, it is perfectly acceptable to pretend you didn't hear them. If you are going for the Parent of the Year Award, you can show up at school with the snacks before second hour. Your choice. If it happens a second time, they didn't learn anything the first time.

Surviving Teenagers Tip # 43- The more control your teen has over their schedule, the better your life will be. There. I said it. You will have NO control once they are off to college. Let them screw up in high school.

Surviving Teenagers Tip # 44- You can tell what kind of home life some teenagers have by how they treat their fellow students. I have seen some of the cruelest behavior on the high school level. Your teenager is faced with this kind of behavior every day. Make sure they are not the ones taking it to school from your home. We made every effort to make our home a haven for our teens, where they could come to get away from the stress in their lives. We didn't allow harsh words and fighting. As parents, we did not argue with each other, we talked it out as a model for the kids to follow. Sure, we blew it occasionally, but we did it right enough times to show the kids how it should be done.

Surviving Teenagers Tip # 45- Sometimes you can bring up sensitive subjects by relating what happened when YOU were in high school. These can be great bonding moments and it puts you into a conversation your teenager would normally be having with their peers. You can't live your life through them, but you can share part of your life with them.

Surviving Teenagers Tip # 46- Google is your friend. When in doubt, Google it. Most parents don't like to be 'schooled' by their kids, or left in the dark about what is going on. The more you know about current teen culture, the better.

Surviving Teenagers Tip # 47- It's a good idea to let five or ten minutes slide when your teenager is late getting home for their curfew, providing they call you before the deadline. Five or ten minutes late is better that an 80 mile per hour race by your teen driver to make it home before the clock strikes the hour.

Surviving Teenagers Tip #48- Choose your battles, and pick the ones you can win. For example, let your teenagers choose their own hair length, nail color, etc. Those are battles you won't win. Teens take these decisions personally, and they expect to have control over their own bodies. In the big scheme of things, it really doesn't matter. (You can also use the photographs to embarrass them later in life.)

Surviving Teenagers Tip #49- Parents, and especially dads, should set an example, and set the standard high. The best thing you can do for your teenager is to live the example you expect them to follow. For instance: After dinner, take your dinner plate into the kitchen and start loading the dishwasher. This, of course, is the last thing you really want to do after a stressful day at work, but take my word for it- It's worth the trouble. Your relationship with your wife and with your kids will improve for the price of ten minutes a night after dinner. Anything you expect them to do, you have to model. In most cases, your kids will follow your lead. When they don't, a friendly request for help can get them moving in the right direction.

Surviving Teenagers Tip #50- Whoever does the laundry gets to keep any money they find in the pockets. I think it's a good rule, my wife disagrees.

Surviving Teenagers Tip # 51- Nothing tells your kids that they are important to you like attending their school activities and sporting events. The time you spend sitting in the stands is like putting money in the bank. One of my biggest regrets is not doing more of this.

"Most of the other parents actually watch the games, mom."

Surviving Teenagers Tip # 52- When you are negotiating and you give your teenager two choices, make sure you can live with both of them.

Surviving Teenagers Tip # 53- Be prepared. You should not expect, "I love you, too," every time you say, "I love you." It is much better to get a sincere "I love you" once a month that an "I love you" every day through clenched teeth.

Surviving Teenagers Tip # 54- Don't get discouraged when your "I love you" is not returned. Keep it up. They hear it and cherish it, even when they are mad at you. And sneak in a hug every chance you get. If you are a family of huggers, your children will be immune to most of the teenage pitfalls. There will be phases your kids go through where they do not respond, or they reject your physical affection outright. Don't take it personally. It's what you do when you are a teenager. They feel the warmth, even if they throw off the blanket.

Surviving Teenagers Tip # 55- You can't pick your teenager's friends. All you can hope for is that some of your child rubs off on them.

Surviving Teenagers Tip # 56- If you are ordering your teenagers around, you are telling them they can't think for themselves. Besides, they won't follow your 'orders' any better than you would follow theirs. The teen years are their transition period before becoming adults. Teenagers deserve an adult dose of respect. If you want a teenager to do what you want, a respectful question is the best way to go. "Would you mind doing _____?" or "Can you help with _____?" or "Would you be willing to _____?" works better than- "Do this!" or "Do that!" Use what works if you want to get something done. You still hold all the cards. If they say no, find out why they can't or won't help. Remind them of this the next time they want something from you. Don't threaten them with retribution if they don't help. They don't usually listen until they want something anyway.

"Oh hi, son. It's Mom again."

Surviving Teenagers Tip # 57- A few tips on divorce. It is better for a child to come from a broken home than to live in one. I really believe that. If you are staying together "for the sake of the kids", really stay together and love each other. Counselling is worth every penny, and teens are too perceptive to be fooled. The teenage time period is the worst possible time for kids to suffer a divorce. They have too many changes going on already.

Surviving Teenagers Tip # 58- A sure way to get your teenager to hate you is to say mean things about their other parent, whom they love, no matter what they've done to you. It's just like badmouthing their friends.

Surviving Teenagers Tip # 59- Teenagers are smarter about relationships than you think. What you might consider a big issue between you and your former spouse will mean nothing to you or your child once they turn eighteen. Be the bigger person. The time goes by fast, so don't miss it or mess it up.

"I wish I could help, dad, but the only engines
I know anything about are search engines."

Surviving Teenagers Tip # 60- Keeping your teenager out of you and your former spouse's business is the best way to show them that they are not to blame for the divorce. Teenagers are mostly focused on themselves. They think everything is their fault. Make sure they know that your problems are not caused by them.

Surviving Teenagers Tip # 61- Teenagers are resilient. They have to be to make it through high school. Unconditional love and acceptance from their parents is the only thing that keeps them firmly grounded. Without it, making it through the teen years is pure luck.

Surviving Teenagers Tip # 62- Everyone gets wronged in a divorce. Suck it up and quit using your teenager as your therapist. Let them use you as THEIR therapist. Or better yet, go see a good therapist on your own or together. It's time and money well spent.

Surviving Teenagers Tip # 63- Don't allow your friends to bad mouth your former spouse in front of your kids. See tip #58. You can exchange your complaints with your friends in private or when you are alone with your therapist, who also happens to be a good listener and is sworn to secrecy.

Surviving Teenagers Tip # 64- A family is a group of people who are committed to each other, and accept each other, no matter what. If your child is unsure about your commitment to their well-being, or they feel like they are criticized too frequently, they will be drawn to another group that resembles a 'family', such as a gang, a cult or a girlfriend or boyfriend. These groups accept new members with open arms. Given a choice, teenagers (and everyone else, for that matter) spend time where they are most accepted.

"Let's pretend we're the family
in the Christmas letter."

Surviving Teenagers Tip # 65- When my youngest son was thirteen, he wanted to get his ear pierced. Getting a boys ear pierced is not a big thing, but I didn't want him to do something permanent like that to himself until he was older and could make a better decision. I told him that if I were going to agree to him getting his ear pierced, he would have to wear a skirt around the house. He is now nineteen and away at college. He hasn't had his ears pierced...yet.

Surviving Teenagers Tip # 66- Refuse to argue with your child. This is a tough one, but it becomes an art form after a while. There are at least two reasons not to argue. (1) You won't win, and (2) You will damage your relationship. When your teenager makes a ridiculous statement, like: "You don't love me anymore," or "You never buy me anything I want," or my personal favorite, "Please, please, PLEASE???," don't panic. When this happens, try to say as sincerely as you can- "I'm really sorry about that," "How sad for you!" or "Nice try, kiddo." Repeat as necessary.

Surviving Teenagers Tip # 67- You don't have to jump every time your teenager 'needs' something. Unless it is something that improves their health or their performance in school, it's much better if you help them figure out a way for them to get what they want by themselves, without expecting someone else to get it for them.

"You can't get your belly button pierced.
I haven't cut the cord yet."

Surviving Teenagers Tip # 68- Pull out the old photographs from when you were a teenager from time to time. Things don't seem so bad when you are reviewing how you used to wear your clothes/hair/nails and the cars you used to drive.

Surviving Teenagers Tip # 69- It is tempting to shoot down ridiculous statements that teenagers make. Teens are in the process of formulating their own political and religious views. They are not rejecting you and your beliefs, they are exploring. Find out exactly what they mean when they start spouting their half-thought-out philosophy. If you reserve judgment and hear them out, you will have an opportunity to give them your views and why you hold them. Remind them that you listened to them when they interrupt you.

Surviving Teenagers Tip # 70- Teenagers with good grades usually got a 'pass' on a lot of the trivial conflicts that arose in our house. We considered school performance to be the teenager's 'job,' and allowed more freedoms when they were responsible with their grades.

Surviving Teenagers Tip # 71- If you have more than one teenager, keep in mind that they do not need to be treated equally. They each have their own strengths and weaknesses. They all need to be treated uniquely, to address the differences they each have.

Surviving Teenagers Tip # 72- If you raise more than one teenager, it is likely that you are going to have one that you are particularly close to, and one that you can't be far enough away from. What I've discovered is that these (perfectly normal) feelings of favoritism may change as your children go through their lives. For Example, you might dread one child's teen years, but you could get along beautifully once they are older. It happened to us. Don't write them off.

Surviving Teenagers Tip # 73- It is important not to play favorites. You can have a favorite, you just won't survive the others if they know about it. It will require extra effort and some brutally honest self-examination to recognize it, but you can work to overcome it.

Surviving Teenagers Tip # 74- So you have a teenager that likes video games? You can still spend time with them by sitting and watching. The first few times you do this, take a pencil with you to bite on. (Don't use a pen, see tip #10) Don't judge what's going on in the game, (it's too late anyways, if they are already playing it) and don't make suggestions until you understand the game. Spend 30 minutes and then leave the room. Do the same thing for a few days. You might be surprised when they actually start talking to you!

Surviving Teenagers Tip # 75- We controlled what video games and movies the children played and watched by controlling what was purchased. We simply didn't buy games we couldn't tolerate.

Surviving Teenagers Tip # 76- Children with problems should not be treated as problem children. Most families have a child that requires extra attention. Sickness, injuries, emotional problems or handicaps require more attention than an 'average' teenager gets. All children, and especially young adults, need to know that they are 'okay' people, and that they are so much more than the total of their life challenge or handicap. Everyone should be made to feel like they can contribute to the family, and everyone in the family should be willing to contribute to the care of the most challenged child.

Surviving Teenagers Tip # 77- The very opposite is also true. Teenagers can feel neglected if another sibling has a special challenge that requires the parent's attention. They don't have to always be Mr. or Miss Perfect all the time because their sibling requires extra care. In fact, it is likely the other child will act out for attention. (Remember, they live on their own planet) Parents need to be aware that the 'normal' child might feel neglected. Make a solid effort to spend comparable time with each teenager.

Surviving Teenagers Tip # 78- Don't get sucked into your teenager's fights. Make them work it out. Don't tolerate them hurting each other of course, but make them talk it out and arrive at a solution. Tell them if you have to provide the solution, it will be one that neither of them will like.

Surviving Teenagers Tip # 79- Sometimes, the best thing to do is to do nothing.

Surviving Teenagers Tip # 80- There are so many changes that teenagers go through between the ages of thirteen and eighteen, that they are essentially new people when they are done. They don't look the same, they don't sound the same, they don't behave the same, and they don't think the same. Parents become convinced of this when they realize there is a stranger in their house.

Surviving Teenagers Tip # 81- Try to be relaxed about a teenager's eating habits. They eat like Hobbits. Breakfast, second breakfast, and on and on. You won't realize how much they ate until they leave for college and you see how much food you have to throw out in left-overs.

Surviving Teenagers Tip # 82- It is hard to know which the bigger crisis is in a teenager's typical drama-filled day. A popped quiz and a popped pimple both present their own unique challenges.

Surviving Teenagers Tip # 83- If you are a dad, you have to set your logical mind aside sometimes. Teenagers rarely say what they mean. Listen for what they MEANT to say. Sometimes "I hate you!" means "I'm scared and you can't help me!" Sometimes it means they hate you. But they really don't. Usually.

Surviving Teenagers Tip # 84- Every kid wants their dad's approval. If you are thought of as a strict disciplinarian, you've got some work to do. Compliments don't come naturally to us. Look for the silver lining, but compliment your kids every time you find a bronze one.

Surviving Teenagers Tip # 85- Teenagers already know right from wrong. Parenting a teenager is not about teaching right and wrong. It is about loosening the apron strings a little bit at a time so your child can experiment with adulthood, while still having a solid home foundation to fall back on if needed. I envy mother birds. Toss 'em a worm and throw them out.

Surviving Teenagers Tip # 86- Since Plato, every generation of teenagers has listened to crappy music. Except our generation, of course.

Surviving Teenagers Tip # 87- You can't control your teenager's behavior. All you can do is control how you react to their behavior. Here's a hypothetical situation- You think your teenager might have stolen something from the mall. You're not sure. You suspect they may have snuck something into their bag the last time you took them shopping. What should you do? Right or wrong, this is what we did. We never took them back to the mall. Since shoplifting is a crime of opportunity, we removed the opportunity. We decided not to confront them or accuse them because we didn't want to weaken our mutual trust or harm our relationship if we were wrong. If they do it again on their own, they might get caught and suffer the natural consequences on their own.

Surviving Teenagers Tip # 88- When you try to tell a teenager something, you may have to rephrase what you are saying and repeat it. They have a completely different understanding of some words, and they only hear what they want to hear. When you actually get to talk to them, you may find glaring gaps in their knowledge of some subjects. Don't be alarmed. They were learning how to swing a bat in little league just a few years ago.

Surviving Tecnagers Tip # 89- Don't fool yourself into thinking that you know what your teenager is thinking. You don't. You just don't.

"I don't know why my parents are depressed. I'm here to check on them all the time."

Surviving Teenagers Tip # 90- If your teenager is musically inclined, encourage them to join the marching band. High school is a whole lot easier when you are starting your freshman year with dozens of friends from summer band camp.

Surviving Teenagers Tip # 91- If you continue to keep the same tight controls on your teenager as you did when they were little, they are not going to be able to think for themselves. They might continue to follow all of your rules, or they more than likely will rebel against them, but they will not be able to think for themselves or make good decisions on their own.

Surviving Teenagers Tip # 92- I think most teenagers make good choices. Even when they make a bad one, most of the other choices being made are good ones. Compliment the good ones if you want your teens to make more good choices. If you have to crack down on a bad choice, compliment the good ones that they made that day.

Surviving Teenagers Tip # 93- Teenagers need their own space. It can be a basement, a bedroom, a garage, or a treehouse, but they need an "alone" place. If your teenager has to share a bedroom, look hard to make another place that one of the kids can escape to. Spreading activity areas around your house will keep teens from getting in each other's way.

"Mom, Dad, when are you
going to get your own place?"

Surviving Teenagers Tip # 94- A surviving marriage between stepdads and stepmoms is a miracle. When you marry your stepchildren's parent, you are killing their dream of their biological parents ever getting back together. Step kids will grieve and be sad, and they won't know why. Expect them to cause problems and pit one parent against the other, and one set of kids against the other.

Surviving Teenagers Tip # 95- Don't cry over spilt milk. It's not just an old expression, it is practical advice. Accidents are going to happen at the dinner table, with all the elbows, drinks and activity. Expect them to happen and be ready. Broken dishes are the same deal. One of the parents should jump up and isolate the area and do the cleanup, if there is broken glass. This helps reinforce the protective nature of parents in the teenager's eyes and sets a good example about what people should and shouldn't get mad about. Angry words are not allowed during cleanup.

"You missed a spot."

Surviving Teenagers Tip # 96- There will come a time when your teenager is going to make you mad and you are going to yell at them. Just so you know ahead of time. You will also feel guilty about it later. Try to avoid it if you can.

Surviving Teenagers Tip # 97- Failure to prepare on a teenager's part does not constitute an emergency on your part. Let natural consequences be the teacher whenever you can. We would like to be, but we are not always going to be there to bail them out.

Surviving Teenagers Tip # 98- Ten minutes alone with a hot beverage has been compared to the sweet, relaxing feeling of a cool evening's breeze. It can also bring your temperature down a few degrees. This is where a locked closet comes in handy. You can thank me later.

Surviving Teenagers Tip # 99- Surprise your teenagers once in a while. Just a little note, or maybe a quick sketch, a compliment or a written joke can really break the ice with a teenager. Don't be afraid to apologize or admit you made a mistake by note when your teenager won't talk to you. Your relationship is changing from parent-kid to mutual respect between two adults. It's not a smooth process.

Surviving Teenagers Tip # 100- Teenagers think they know it all, just like you did when you were a teenager. It is impossible to convince them otherwise. As your teenager gains more life experience, and they discover all they haven't learned yet, they will appreciate all you know even more.

I saved this one for last, but it's one of the most important.

Surviving Teenagers Tip #101- Say YES, unless there's a good reason to say NO. "I'm too tired", or "I don't want to", are not valid reasons to say no to your kids at any age. Suck it up and act like a parent. Parenting, and especially parenting teenagers, is not for sissies.

Thanks for reading!

I hope you enjoyed this book as much as I enjoyed writing it. If you wouldn't mind, could you take a moment and write a few words and review this book? Favorable reviews are essential for writers and it really makes us motivated to write more. Thanks a lot!

Discover Kurt Zimmerman's other books at:

http://www.amazon.com/-/e/B00711L4QK

Or at Kurt's website:

http://www.kurtwzimmerman.com

About the author-

Kurt Zimmerman, as a father of seven, and a step-father to five, enjoys writing books and crafting stories for and about his own family. He has also spent many years writing newsletters and policy manuals for a chain of retail stores, where he is currently vice president and director of operations. In his spare time(?) he builds movie props and makes public appearances with his full-sized Star Wars R2D2, C1-10P and BB-8 replicas, raising money for charities and entertaining children and grownups alike.

Printed in Great Britain
by Amazon.co.uk, Ltd.,
Marston Gate.